ZB

CW00666746

1,000,000 Books

are available to read at

www.ForgottenBooks.com

Read online
Download PDF
Purchase in print

ISBN 978-0-428-80063-5
PIBN 11299323

This book is a reproduction of an important historical work. Forgotten Books uses
state-of-the-art technology to digitally reconstruct the work, preserving the original format
whilst repairing imperfections present in the aged copy. In rare cases, an imperfection in
the original, such as a blemish or missing page, may be replicated in our edition. We do,
however, repair the vast majority of imperfections successfully; any imperfections that
remain are intentionally left to preserve the state of such historical works.

Forgotten Books is a registered trademark of FB &c Ltd.
Copyright © 2018 FB &c Ltd.
FB &c Ltd, Dalton House, 60 Windsor Avenue, London, SW19 2RR.
Company number 08720141. Registered in England and Wales.

For support please visit www.forgottenbooks.com

1 MONTH OF
FREE
READING

at
www.ForgottenBooks.com

By purchasing this book you are eligible for one month membership to ForgottenBooks.com, giving you unlimited access to our entire collection of over 1,000,000 titles via our web site and mobile apps.

To claim your free month visit:
www.forgottenbooks.com/free1299323

* Offer is valid for 45 days from date of purchase. Terms and conditions apply.

English
Français
Deutsche
Italiano
Español
Português

www.forgottenbooks.com

Mythology Photography **Fiction**
Fishing Christianity **Art** Cooking
Essays Buddhism Freemasonry
Medicine **Biology** Music **Ancient**
Egypt Evolution Carpentry Physics
Dance Geology **Mathematics** Fitness
Shakespeare **Folklore** Yoga Marketing
Confidence Immortality Biographies
Poetry **Psychology** Witchcraft
Electronics Chemistry History **Law**
Accounting **Philosophy** Anthropology
Alchemy Drama Quantum Mechanics
Atheism Sexual Health **Ancient History**
Entrepreneurship Languages Sport
Paleontology Needlework Islam
Metaphysics Investment Archaeology
Parenting Statistics Criminology
Motivational

An Eye Case in the Courts:

Charles Archibald

BY

C. A. ROBERTSON, A. M. (Harvard), M. D.,

Fellow of the Massachusetts Medical Society, Member of the American Ophthalmological Society, Delegate to the Medical Society of the State of New York, Ophthalmic and Aural Surgeon at St. Peter's Hospital, Albany, and at the Troy and Cohoes Hospitals.

"NO PLEASURE IS COMPARABLE TO THE STANDING UPON THE VANTAGE GROUND OF TRUTH."—*Bacon.*

c

ALBANY:
THE ARGUS COMPANY, PRINTERS.
1873.

An Eye Case in the Courts:

Charles Archibald

BY

C. A. ROBERTSON, A. M. (Harvard), M. D.,

Fellow of the Massachusetts Medical Society, Member of the American Ophthalmological Society, Delegate to the Medical Society of the State of New York, Ophthalmic and Aural Surgeon at St. Peter's Hospital, Albany, and at the Troy and Cohoes Hospitals.

"No Pleasure is Comparable to the Standing upon the Vantage Ground of Truth."—*Bacon.*

---

c

ALBANY:

THE ARGUS COMPANY, PRINTERS.

1873.

HARVARD UNIVERSITY
SCHOOL OF MEDICINE AND PUBLIC HEALTH
LIBRARY

28.D.1873.3

1873, July 12.
Gift of
Sam'l A. Green, M.D.
of Boston.
(H. U. 1851.)

AN EYE CASE IN THE COURTS.

JOHN C. TINNEY *agt.* THE NEW JERSEY STEAMBOAT COMPANY.

The following is one of a series of cases in practice contained in a paper presented to the New York State Medical Society at the last meeting, February, 1873, and it is one that has become somewhat noted in law as the case of John C. Tinney against the New Jersey Steamboat Company. The action was commenced by plaintiff for alleged damages in the sum of $15,000 for impairment of sight, the result of alleged injury received on the Hudson river steamboat, Dean Richmond.

Tinney, a man about twenty-eight years old, called to consult me the 24th September, 1867, at the instance of his family physician, Dr. Witbeck of West Troy. He complained* of great indistinctness of vision, which he referred to an injury on the brow done by a slat of a steamboat berth, breaking under the weight of an occupant above him, as the boat struck the pier forcibly when arriving at Albany on the morning of April 21st, ult. The broken extremity, he said, struck him over the left eye and held him impaled until the person above him got out of his berth. He said that the wound bled, and blood settled all around the eye and the lids were afterward swollen shut, but that the eyeball itself was not struck. At the time of consulting me, he said that

he could not distinguish a person's features a yard off
so as to recognize the person when the right eye was
closed ; and could only count the number of fingers held
up before him.

On inspection I saw a small linear scar over the inner
extremity of the eyebrow. This scar was a white
cicatrix and clearly an old affair. No signs of recent
injury existed. The ophthalmoscope revealed a degree
of congenital hypermetropia, but no morbid products.
The action of the pupil was normal and the tension of
the globe also.

As the patient did not develop an ulterior purpose
in consulting me, I did not suspect any deception in his
statements relative to inability to see well, and I inti-
mated to him that his impairment of vision, the degree
of which I did not seek to accurately determine, might
have been caused by an injury done to a branch of one
of the fifth pair of nerves. He seemed very curious as
to this opinion, and asked a good many questions regard-
ing it.

I suggested that time might remedy his hurt, but
doubted the efficacy of any treatment. Two months
afterward, he came again to see me, and then informed
me that he intended to bring an action at law for
damages, and I was subsequently served with a *subpœna*
to appear as a medical witness. I then felt a misgiving
as to his credibility, and requested him not to subpœna
me for reasons that I stated. He remarked that I had
referred to the case of Dr. C., when he first consulted me,
who was thrown from his carriage, striking violently on
his head, the sight becoming impaired by consequence,.

although the eye was not struck ; and that neither I nor subsequently another oculist, Dr. Hinton of New York, could detect anything wrong in the eye ; and that this was too like his own case, and too important for his benefit, not to be brought before the jury. Therefore, he insisted upon summoning me as a witness.

The case was not reached on the calendar until another term of the court, when I was again subpœnaed. At this time, when Tinney. called to summon me, I affected sufficient interest in his case to secure an oppor-' tunity to satisfy my mind as to the correctness of my suspicions that he could really see better than he pretended. The ophthalmoscope revealed nothing more than at first. I tried various experiments with prisms, lenses, test-type and test-objects,. and I found his answers to my questions conflicting ; but the experiment with a stereoscope settled the question of his falseness beyond a per adventure.

Upon a card prepared for the purpose, I had pasted, at the proper distance apart, these characters :

CENTS   12 1-2

(= No. 7 of Snellen's test-type), cut from a newspaper-heading. Now, the action of light upon the glasses, or prisms of the stereoscope produces an optical illusion, so that what is seen by the right eye appears to be on the left side, and *vice versa*, and the separatrix between the prisms prevents either eye from seeing what is before the other. Accordingly, an apparent transformation of the characters above mentioned would be effected to the eyes of an ordinary observer, and he would read it twelve and a half cents.

I carefully placed the stereoscope, with the card adjusted in front of the prisms, before the eyes of Tinney for a moment, telling him not to wink. On its removal, I asked him what he saw. He promptly replied that he saw "twelve and a half cents." I said, "that is right," and placed the instrument on my desk, when he added, "the figures were blurred, but I could see they were figures." Unfortunately for the victim of this optical illusion, the *figures*, which he said seemed *blurred*, were in front of his well eye (the right), although apparently on the left of the word *cents*, and could be seen *only* by the well eye; while the word *cents*, respecting which he made complaint as lacking in distinctness, was in front of his alleged bad eye (the left), and could be seen *only* by the left eye! The fair inference from his remark as to the blurring was that the sight of his damaged eye was better than that of the sound one!

Before the trial the attorneys, both for the plaintiff and for the defendant, called on me. The latter stated that he had made an offer to Tinney to compensate him for any injury he had received, if he would have the degree of impairment of sight resulting from the injury determined by the examination of some fair and competent oculist; but the offer was rejected by the advice of counsel. He continued, that he had heard that I was subpœnaed by Tinney, and desired to ascertain my relation to the case. I told him that I was averse to appearing in court at all in the matter; that I was indifferent as to the parties at issue, and would not appear as a partisan, but simply as a scientific witness. Thereupon he expressed his satisfaction and left.

The attorney and counsel for the plaintiff asked me, at their interview, if I could tell by examination and experiment with glasses the condition of the sight, to which I replied affirmatively. They made no allusion to my examination of their client, and experiments with glasses to determine the condition of his sight. But they omitted to call me on the witness stand, at the trial, although they had subpœnaed me !

I was, however, called on the stand by the attorney for the defense, and I stated various methods of examination which I had employed with prisms, test-type and other objects. I explained the crucial test which I had made, and exhibited the stereoscope and card.

Tinney himself appeared as a witness, and the facts were established, that he had suffered from granular lids, and his father before him, and both had undergone medical treatment for the disease.

His family physician, Dr. Witbeck, testified in the case, but neither the latter, nor Tinney himself, spoke of any violence except on the brow. The doctor's treatment was directed solely to the bruise there and to the accompanying tumefaction and ecchymosis about the lids.

Daniel Webster is said to have expressed an irreverent doubt if divine intelligence could forecast what verdict a jury would render; and in this case the jury, regardless of scientific and indubitable proof to the contrary, awarded the plaintiff damages in the sum of $5,000 for injury done to his sight; and this, too, upon the uncorroborated statement of the interested party himself, who wanted $15,000.

The case, however, was carried up on appeal to the

General Term of the Supreme Court. Hon. John H. Reynolds argued it before the full bench, and explained the experiment by which the plaintiff's vision had been tested, and exhibited the stereoscope and card to the judges, who verified the experiment. The case was sent back by the court for new trial at the Circuit on the ground of excessive damages.

The new trial took place May 22d, 1872, nearly five years after my examination of the eye.

The novel feature of this trial was the testimony of Dr. George T. Stevens, who appeared as a witness for the plaintiff. This witness stated that he was a professor at the Albany Medical College, and asserted that he had examined the plaintiff's eye on the 20th of March, 1872, and found that with the left eye he read No. 8, Snellen's test-type, at twelve inches, "without a glass;" thus indicating one-eighth ($\frac{1}{8}$) of perfect vision. He testified that with $\frac{1}{12}$ convex glass the plaintiff read Nos. 6, 8 and 10, which is tantamount to saying that he saw a larger object (No. 10) with a *magnifying* glass than he saw without one, and also that he saw one a little smaller, too! The witness further deposed that he next tried prisms before the patient's eyes, in order "to satisfy" himself, and from the patient's answers he was satisfied that there was "a defect of vision in the left eye." He asserted that "a person not an expert could not judge" which image was seen through the prism and which by the naked eye, and he expressed a "doubt whether an expert could." Any intelligent person, however, may readily satisfy himself how entirely unwarranted such an assertion is, by looking steadily at an object, and then interposing a prism before one of his eyes, for he will instantaneously recognize the utter fallaciousnes of the experiment as a conclusive test of deception, and perceive how easily, by means of it, a practiced malingerer, hungry for money, could impose on an inexperienced examiner. In this case, the plaintiff had enjoyed a favorable opportunity to become familiar with the action of prisms, for his attorney had borrowed of me, and kept for several weeks, the stereoscope exhibited at thefirst trial.

Next, the deponent said he "used a diagram used by oculists," "made in the form of a wheel with spokes," the spokes "composed of three distinct lines."* (The diagram referred to was undoubtedly one of the astigmatic† tests of my friend, Dr. John Green of St. Louis, proposed to the American Ophthalmological Society at our session at Niagara Falls in 1867. The three lines of the spokes correspond in width to No. 20‾ of Snellen's test-types. These tests, photographed on glass, were well shown to the State Society last year, with a magic lantern, by our accomplished *confrère*, Dr. Noyes of New York.) Witness testified that at a distance of twenty feet, Tinney "could not make out anything" with the left eye. He then "brought it within six feet and he (plaintiff) said he could see certain lines better than cer-

---

* NOTE.—The quotations of testimony in this case are copied from the court reporter's stenographic minutes.

† DEFINITION.—For the general reader, it may be stated that when the eye is misshapen in front, so that rays of light falling on it are not brought to a common focal point within the eye-ball, then the eye is said to be focusless, or *astigmatic*. The properly shaped cornea, or front of the eye, is almost uniformly curved (for example, like the end of an egg), while the astigmatic eye may have curvatures that differ as the curves on the side of an egg, that is those on its long diameter from those on the short diameter.

tain other lines." .Now if the vague word "within" was used, as it seems to be, with the import of the phrase *in the neighborhood of*, then it would seem that the left eye had visual power equal to *about* $\frac{6}{20}$ i. e., *about* $\frac{1}{3}$ of perfect vision in certain meridians. As his previous experiments with test-type had demonstrated that the unaided left eye possessed only $\frac{1}{8}$ of perfect vision in all meridians, then $\frac{1}{8}$ was the visual power in the most faulty meridian, and the difference between $\frac{1}{8}$ and $\frac{6}{20}$ (about) i. e., $\frac{1}{6}$ represents the degree of astigmatism which must have existed according to this witness.

The witness said he further proceeded as follows: "directing him to look downward as much as possible and bringing these lines a little nearer, I found he could see the lines a little better." It would have been more remarkable, if he had *not* seen them better when brought nearer; but how Dr. Stevens anticipated at this stage of his investigation that plaintiff could see better by looking "downward as much as possible," when it was not till *afterward* that he detected a condition in the eye (as he goes on to declare), the discovery of which would have been likely to prompt him to direct his patient to look downward, is passing strange! Witness went on next to explain how he *subsequently* acquired the information which he had *previously* made use of. It seems like the goose hatching the gosling, and afterwards laying the egg which produced it! For he says that, by means of the ophthalmoscope, he afterwards found that he could see well through the upper part of the cornea when patient was *looking downwards*. I prefer to quote the exact language, in order to do no injustice to this testimony, which was apparently dovetailed for the occasion, and, however crude it may seem to the scientific mind, doubtless had a value in the opinion of the "professor." With the aid of the ophthalmoscope, as he testified, he *"found the retina devoid of any indications of disease;" "could see the upper and lower borders of the disc were less distinct than the borders upon each side;" "the small horizontal vessels could be seen by effort;" "causing plaintiff to look forward, throwing this beam of light* (i. e., from the ophthalmoscope) *through the lower part of the cornea, I found the image of the retina was extremely indistinct and greatly distorted; everything about the retina was extremely indistinct and greatly distorted; everything about the retina seemed to be distorted and irregular; it was difficult to make out anything distintly;" "causing him to look down, and throwing the beam through the upper part of the cornea, there was more distinctness; I could make out everything quite clear in the interior of the eye then; I could see that the horizontal vessels existed then, and were as clear as the others."* Here transpires the *anticipated* reason for directing the plaintiff to look downward, which was noted above as remarkable! But the *law of visible direction* did not seem to be known to this expert witness, according to which all objects are seen in the lines of direction that intersect at the optical center of the eye, whether the eye is turned upward or downward in looking directly at an object; and it did not seem to be known by him that the cornea is not a "periscopic" glass, and that no one can elect to look *directly* through the upper or the lower part of his cornea at will.

It follows, therefore, that it could not be true that the direction in which the eyes were turned improved the sight of the plaintiff in looking *at* the three lines.

In reply to the questions, "have you stated all your tests?" and, "what was your conclusion?" deponent answered "*that there was irregularity of the curvature of the cornea, more especially of the lower portion; the upper portion is not free entirely, but comparatively free from this curvature; the lower portion is entirely distorted.*" "*The effect upon the sight would be to render all images indistinct.*" "*The disease was astigmatism.*" "*Astigmatism may be natural or may be acquired; regular astigmatisms are natural; an irregular astigmatism is usually acquired; this was an irregular astigmatism.*" Further on the witness responded "*yes*" to the question, "I understood you that this *irregular astigmatism is* ALMOST INVARIABLY *caused by inflammation?*" He also answered "*yes*" to the question, "and that inflammation may arise from an accident?"

Prof. Donders says "astigmatism is either congenital or acquired; in the great majority of cases it is congenital." (See Sydenham Society, vol. xxii, p. 511.) Also, irregular astigmatism may be divided into normal and abnormal. The normal form is connected with the structure of the lens; the cornea does not participate in producing it." (P. 543.) Abnormal astigmatism refers to the degree of the defect interfering with perfect vision, for a slight degree of astigmatism is the common, or normal condition of all eyes. In every forty or fifty cases, without exaggeration, one is, in consequence of astigmatism, disturbed in its function. Now in a disagreement between the eminent Utrecht authority, just quoted, and Dr. Stevens, involving the relative frequency of acquired astigmatism, and the way in which it is "*almost invariably caused*," the latter would be an *imponderable*.

The case, without other medical testimony than already mentioned, was committed to the jury. The result was another curious exemplification of the impossibility of divining the judgment of a jury. No verdict was rendered, the jury disagreeing on the point of the company being responsible for an accident, against which, it was contended, all care and diligence had been exercised. Consequently a third trial was made necessary.

During the last session of the State Medical Society, the third trial was going on, and this paper has since been completed.

Fresh interest was added to the case by the appearance of Dr. Agnew, the president of the Society.

It was clear that the plaintiff and his counsel, with or without some new conditions of the eye, had recovered from the original aversion to examination of the eye by oculists !

Dr. Agnew testified that he examined the eye, "three or four weeks ago, in the way we usually do when we desire to find out if an eye is healthy or not." The witness did not state it, but it is competent to mention, that we *usually* assume in private practice that our patients do not intend to impose upon us, otherwise we should properly resort to unusual ways to detect the imposition.

He found a "small, faint spot" on the cornea "which

was in such a position as to interfere with sight." This was a new feature in the case.

He tried various kinds of spectacles, but only got vision of one-tenth. The doctor explained the manner in which the degree of vision is notated by means of test-type.

To the question, "did you satisfy yourself the sight was impaired without taking his statement?" the answer was given, "I did not take his statement; we have means of determining without taking their statements, when the vision of one eye is perfect." Unfortunately, the question was not asked, what means were employed in this case, and — another very important matter — what degree of illumination was used, and the witness did not state. In the instance of an expert impostor, which was the issue raised in this case, all the means actually employed and the precautions against imposition, would have interest and permanent importance.

The witness proceeded to state that in his opinion "the injury [spot?] was permanent." The question followed : "Is there any irregularity except the spot?" which was answered : "that would account for the irregularity." The doctor said that such a defect could be caused by inflammation of the eye. The attorney for plaintiff then proposed a hypothetical case of an exaggerated character, which was not in nature or degree like Tinney's case, as stated to me by himself or Dr. Witbeck, his physician; and then asked if such an inflammation of the eye, as narrated, could cause a defect like Tinney's. The witness properly and inevitably answered, "I think so!"

Upon his cross-examination, the witness testified that he used a single prism in ascertaining the defect of sight, and that "he had to take his statement, of course." He did not use the stereoscope, he said.

The substance of the further testimony of the witness was as follows: "*The chief opacity was a little to the nasal side of the centre;*" "*it was not easily seen by unaided vision;*" "*could not say whether this opacity was recent or not;*" "*it might or might not account for any defect;*" [that is of sight?] "*found slight changes* [nature not stated] *in the choroid coat;*" "*also around the edge of the nerve some slight changes;*" "*the refraction of the eye was not perfectly normal; that condition I supposed to be congenital; I call that hypermetropia;*" "*there was slight astigmatism,*" "*corrected partially by a particular glass;*" "*I found it* (the astigmatism) REGULAR;" "*cannot say how much of his defect of vision is due to some congenital cause, and how much acquired;*" "*an external injury or blow is not a necessary cause to such opacity and such choroidal changes;*" "*might exist simply in the natural course of disease of the eye;*" "*may have no relation to any injury or accident that occurred four or five years ago.*"

The testimony of Dr. Agnew was given frankly and distinctly, and with the manifest intent of communicating what really lay in his own mind. It in no way, however, established the least connection between the accident alleged to have happened in April, 1867, and the condition of things observed by him early in 1873, almost six years afterwards, in a patient, once, if not still subject to ophthalmia, and possessing a congenital defect of sight, which he had only to exaggerate in his representations, in order to successfully deceive any one who relied upon the experiments mentioned by the doctor.

But my test with the stereoscope, again shown in court, was another affair, being made early in the history of the case, before the plaintiff had reason to believe himself suspected of imposture, and had learned the necessity, in order to secure $15,000 from the Steamboat Company, of some familiarity with refracting glasses, and, perhaps, had found a way to produce a "*slight cloudiness*" upon the cornea; and the infallible test was unaffected by all the testimony brought by legal counsel to show that their client ought not to see, when the fact stood incontestable that he did see! It was very like the case of the man, who was told by his lawyer, after stating the statute, "they cannot put you into the stocks." "But, you see," he replied, "I am in the stocks!"

The jury, after this trial, brought in a verdict in behalf of the plaintiff for damages, in the sum of one thousand dollars, which was a mere *bagatelle*, if the jury believed that his sight was damaged to the extent that Tinney alleged, and was excessive if the defect in vision had "no relation to any injury or accident that occurred four or five years before," and was accorded to plaintiff, in order to compensate for loss of time and physicians' fees when he received the bruise.

Dr. Stevens reappeared at this trial, as a witness for plaintiff, and testified that he was a professor in the Albany Medical College; had given attention to diseases of the eye, "*more especially for the last three or four years;*" "*never resided in or made any special course of study at any eye infirmary.*"

He repeated statements made at the former trial; but he developed some curious phases of testimony, so surprising to be found in the utterances of a professed teacher and presumably honest man, that the report of the medical aspect of this case would be incomplete if the testimony were passed over in silence.

The minutes of the court stenographer contain the following questions and remarkable answers, which are copied *verbatim*.

On the cross-examination:

QUESTION. "When you examined plaintiff, the *principal difficulty* you thought you found was astigmatism?"

ANSWER. "*I thought it was; yes.*"

Q. "Was it regular or irregular?"

A. "It was regular in the upper part, but the two parts were not alike."

Q. "Did you call the *principal difficulty* regular or irregular astigmatism?"

A. "REGULAR ASTIGMATISM." [*sic.*] *!!*

Q. "Did you upon the former trial call it regular?"

A. "I PRESUME I DID; *I am not able to remember so as to repeat my evidence at that time.*" *!!*

Q. "I will read from the former trial [*reads*]; did you swear to that?"

A. "*As it is upon the Recorder's minutes, probably I did;* I CANNOT REMEMBER." [*sic.*] *!!*

What was read by the advocate for the steamboat company, was the following from the *direct* testimony of Dr. Stevens, at the former trial, viz.:

Q. "Is there a disease well known to the profession as astigmatism?"

A. "Yes."

Q. "What is it caused by?"

A. "It may be natural or it may be acquired; *regular astigma-*

sion it be urged, that the "professor" was perhaps igno-
rant of the meaning of *irregular astigmatism*. But
whether the perplexity in which he found himself, is to be
regarded as resulting from lack of knowledge, lack of
honesty, or an incredible failure of memory, the stern-
ness of scientific judgment will equally pronounce that
a witness who presumes to appear in court as a scientific
expert, is inexcusable for deliberately falsifying the defi-
nitions of science, in order to free himself from such
meshes as never can entangle intelligence or honesty.

Unjustifiable as the nature of the attempt to escape
was, the baffled witness only multiplied the harassing
contradictions in which he was complicated by making
the futile effort. He said on his *cross*-examination,
respecting the curvature of the cornea, "it was *regular
in the upper part*." On his *direct* examination at the
previous trial, he had said : "there was *irregularity* of
the curvature of the cornea, more especially 'of the lower
part ; the *upper portion is not free* entirely, but comparatively free from this curvature," that is, if the language means anything, the "professor" contradicts himself again, and asserts of the upper part of the cornea
that it *was free* entirely, and *it was not free* entirely of
irregularity ! A strange assertion for a "professor" to
make on oath before an ordinary jury, and it must excite
regret as the mildest emotion of medical judges. The
witness said he had given lectures on the eye to students
"*the last three years*," and had qualified himself by at-
tending to the eye "*more especially the last three or four
years ;*" but such result of learning or teaching (for "by
teaching, one," 'tis said, "may learn to spell") will not

promote the development of science, while it must reflect discredit upon the "professor's" attainments.

But the enumeration is not complete of consequences no less intellectually absurd than morally deprecable, which seem to hound the victim of the unfortunate *failure to remember* (!) what had been his labor to establish at the previous trial, viz. : that the plaintiff was suffering from *irregular* astigmatism, a condition of the eye distinguished from *regular* astigmatism by being, he said, "*almost invariably caused by inflammation*," which an accident, like Tinney's, might have originated, whereas, *regular* astigmatisms are natural," by which he means congenital, for it is a misfortune of the "professor" not to be accurate in what he says.

Continuing the testimony just quoted, the stenographer reports the following language : "In looking through the lower part of the cornea, the irregularity seemed greater than when looking through the upper part." The recorded testimony, which he *did not remember* so as to repeat, was to the same effect, only more emphatic, viz., "through the lower part of the cornea the image was exceedingly distorted;" "everything * * distorted and irregular," *etc.* At both trials, he testified not only to what he professed to have observed with the ophthalmoscope; but he also swore that the plaintiff saw better through the *upper* part of the cornea, where he professed to have found what, by a perversion of terms, he called *regular* astigmatism. Yet, after all this, he swore on his final cross-examination that the *principal defect* in plaintiff's eye was REGULAR *astigmatism !* Then, forsooth, it follows from the testimony of this veracious and scientific expert, that Tinney saw best in that part of his eye where the "principal defect" existed!

But this absurdity is not the only logical sequence of his singular testimony, for he must have seen better also because of the existence of the "principal defect," as well as in the seat of it, if it be true that he saw worse in the lower part of the cornea because of the existence of what was *not* the "principal defect."

But, enough! The pitiful performance is exhibited — the "act, that had no relish of salvation in it," is done, and seen, and judged. Let the kissed book be forgotten, and let the curtain drop, lest there be more fantastic tricks for it to hide.

CPSIA information can be obtained
at www.ICGtesting.com
Printed in the USA
LVHW042232221118
597992LV00017B/329/P

9 780428 800635